THIS CIGAR JOURNAL BELONGS TO:

_____

DEDICATION

This Cigar Journal Log book is dedicated to all the Aficionados out there who love to try & review different cigars and document their findings in the process.

You are my inspiration for producing books and I'm honored to be a part of keeping all of your Cigar notes and records organized.

This journal notebook will help you record your details about tasting cigars.

Thoughtfully put together with these sections to record: Name of Cigar, Brand, Origin, Price, Date, Length/ Ring Size, Buy Again?, Affix Label, Flavor Wheel, Rating, Flavor Strength and Notes.

HOW TO USE THIS BOOK:

The purpose of this book is to keep all of your Cigar notes all in one place. It will help keep you organized.

This Cigar Journal will allow you to accurately document every detail about trying new Cigars. It's a great way to chart your course through smoking Cigars.

Here are examples of the prompts for you to fill in and write about your experience in this book:

1. Name Of Cigar - Write the Name of the Cigar.
2. Brand - Record the Brand.
3. Origin Log where the Cigar was made.
4. Price - For writing the Cost of the Cigar.
5. Date - When did you purchase.
6. Length/ Ring Size - Write the Length and Ring Size.
7. Buy Again? - Would you buy this Cigar again?
8. Affix Label - Place to attach the wrapper.
9. Flavor Wheel - Allows you to record the flavor (linger/ finish, body, leather, oily, bitter, earthy, woody, nutty, chocolate, toffee, vanilla, sweet, spicy, herbal, tropical fruit, dark fruit).
10. Rating - Rate overall with 1-5 stars.
11. Flavor Strength - Full, Medium Full, Medium, Mild, Mellow.
12. Notes - Make note of any other important details

Enjoy!

NAME OF CIGAR _____

BRAND _____ ORIGIN _____

PRICE _____ DATE _____

LENGTH/RING SIZE _____ / _____ BUY AGAIN? _____

AFFIX LABEL HERE

FLAVOR WHEEL

- BODY
- DARK FRUIT
- TROPICAL FRUIT
- HERBAL
- SPICY
- SWEET
- VANILLA
- TOFFEE
- CHOCOLATE
- NUTTY
- WOODY
- EARTHY
- LEATHER
- BITTER
- OILY
- LINGER/FINISH

RATING
☆☆☆☆☆

FLAVOR STRENGTH
- FULL
- MED. FULL
- MEDIUM
- MILD
- MELLOW

NOTES
_____
_____
_____
_____
_____

NAME OF CIGAR _____

BRAND _____ ORIGIN _____

PRICE _____ DATE _____

LENGTH/RING SIZE _____ / _____ BUY AGAIN? _____

```
┌ ─ ─ ─ ─ ─ ─ ─ ─ ─ ─ ─ ─ ─ ─ ─ ─ ─ ─ ─ ─ ─ ─ ─ ─ ─ ─ ┐
                     AFFIX LABEL HERE
└ ─ ─ ─ ─ ─ ─ ─ ─ ─ ─ ─ ─ ─ ─ ─ ─ ─ ─ ─ ─ ─ ─ ─ ─ ─ ─ ┘
```

FLAVOR WHEEL

Axes: BODY, DARK FRUIT, TROPICAL FRUIT, HERBAL, SPICY, SWEET, VANILLA, TOFFEE, CHOCOLATE, NUTTY, WOODY, EARTHY, LEATHER, BITTER, OILY, LINGER/FINISH

Rings: 0.1, 0.2, 0.3, 0.4, 0.5, 0.6

RATING

☆ ☆ ☆ ☆ ☆

FLAVOR STRENGTH

- FULL
- MED. FULL
- MEDIUM
- MILD
- MELLOW

NOTES

_____

_____

_____

_____

_____

NAME OF CIGAR _____

BRAND _____ ORIGIN _____

PRICE _____ DATE _____

LENGTH/RING SIZE _____ / _____ BUY AGAIN? _____

AFFIX LABEL HERE

FLAVOR WHEEL

- BODY
- LINGER/FINISH
- OILY
- BITTER
- LEATHER
- EARTHY
- WOODY
- NUTTY
- CHOCOLATE
- TOFFEE
- VANILLA
- SWEET
- SPICY
- HERBAL
- TROPICAL FRUIT
- DARK FRUIT

RATING

☆☆☆☆☆

FLAVOR STRENGTH

- FULL
- MED. FULL
- MEDIUM
- MILD
- MELLOW

NOTES

_____
_____
_____
_____
_____

NAME OF CIGAR _____

BRAND _____ ORIGIN _____

PRICE _____ DATE _____

LENGTH/RING SIZE _____ / _____ BUY AGAIN? _____

AFFIX LABEL HERE

FLAVOR WHEEL

- BODY
- LINGER/FINISH
- DARK FRUIT
- OILY
- TROPICAL FRUIT
- BITTER
- HERBAL
- LEATHER
- SPICY
- EARTHY
- SWEET
- WOODY
- VANILLA
- NUTTY
- TOFFEE
- CHOCOLATE

RATING

☆ ☆ ☆ ☆ ☆

FLAVOR STRENGTH

- FULL
- MED. FULL
- MEDIUM
- MILD
- MELLOW

NOTES

NAME OF CIGAR _____

BRAND _____ ORIGIN _____

PRICE _____ DATE _____

LENGTH/RING SIZE _____ / _____ BUY AGAIN? _____

AFFIX LABEL HERE

FLAVOR WHEEL

- BODY
- DARK FRUIT
- TROPICAL FRUIT
- HERBAL
- SPICY
- SWEET
- VANILLA
- TOFFEE
- CHOCOLATE
- NUTTY
- WOODY
- EARTHY
- LEATHER
- BITTER
- OILY
- LINGER/FINISH

RATING

☆☆☆☆☆

FLAVOR STRENGTH

- FULL
- MED. FULL
- MEDIUM
- MILD
- MELLOW

NOTES

_____

_____

_____

_____

_____

NAME OF CIGAR _____

BRAND _____ ORIGIN _____

PRICE _____ DATE _____

LENGTH/RING SIZE _____ / _____ BUY AGAIN? _____

AFFIX LABEL HERE

FLAVOR WHEEL

- BODY
- LINGER/FINISH
- OILY
- BITTER
- LEATHER
- EARTHY
- WOODY
- NUTTY
- CHOCOLATE
- TOFFEE
- VANILLA
- SWEET
- SPICY
- HERBAL
- TROPICAL FRUIT
- DARK FRUIT

RATING

☆ ☆ ☆ ☆ ☆

FLAVOR STRENGTH

- FULL
- MED. FULL
- MEDIUM
- MILD
- MELLOW

NOTES

_____

_____

_____

_____

_____

NAME OF CIGAR _____

BRAND _____ ORIGIN _____

PRICE _____ DATE _____

LENGTH/RING SIZE _____ / _____ BUY AGAIN? _____

AFFIX LABEL HERE

FLAVOR WHEEL

- BODY
- LINGER/FINISH
- DARK FRUIT
- OILY
- TROPICAL FRUIT
- BITTER
- HERBAL
- LEATHER
- SPICY
- EARTHY
- SWEET
- WOODY
- VANILLA
- NUTTY
- TOFFEE
- CHOCOLATE

RATING

☆☆☆☆☆

FLAVOR STRENGTH

- FULL
- MED. FULL
- MEDIUM
- MILD
- MELLOW

NOTES

NAME OF CIGAR _____

BRAND _____ ORIGIN _____

PRICE _____ DATE _____

LENGTH/RING SIZE _____/_____ BUY AGAIN? _____

AFFIX LABEL HERE

FLAVOR WHEEL

BODY
LINGER/FINISH — DARK FRUIT
OILY — TROPICAL FRUIT
BITTER — HERBAL
LEATHER — SPICY
EARTHY — SWEET
WOODY — VANILLA
NUTTY — TOFFEE
CHOCOLATE

RATING

☆ ☆ ☆ ☆ ☆

FLAVOR STRENGTH

FULL
MED. FULL
MEDIUM
MILD
MELLOW

NOTES

_____
_____
_____
_____
_____

NAME OF CIGAR _____

BRAND _____ ORIGIN _____

PRICE _____ DATE _____

LENGTH/RING SIZE _____ / _____ BUY AGAIN? _____

AFFIX LABEL HERE

FLAVOR WHEEL

- BODY
- LINGER/FINISH
- DARK FRUIT
- OILY
- TROPICAL FRUIT
- BITTER
- HERBAL
- LEATHER
- SPICY
- EARTHY
- SWEET
- WOODY
- VANILLA
- NUTTY
- TOFFEE
- CHOCOLATE

RATING

☆ ☆ ☆ ☆ ☆

FLAVOR STRENGTH

- FULL
- MED. FULL
- MEDIUM
- MILD
- MELLOW

NOTES

_____

_____

_____

_____

_____

NAME OF CIGAR _____

BRAND _____ ORIGIN _____

PRICE _____ DATE _____

LENGTH/RING SIZE _____ / _____ BUY AGAIN? _____

AFFIX LABEL HERE

FLAVOR WHEEL

- BODY
- DARK FRUIT
- TROPICAL FRUIT
- HERBAL
- SPICY
- SWEET
- VANILLA
- TOFFEE
- CHOCOLATE
- NUTTY
- WOODY
- EARTHY
- LEATHER
- BITTER
- OILY
- LINGER/FINISH

RATING
☆ ☆ ☆ ☆ ☆

FLAVOR STRENGTH
- FULL
- MED. FULL
- MEDIUM
- MILD
- MELLOW

NOTES
_____
_____
_____
_____
_____

NAME OF CIGAR _____

BRAND _____ ORIGIN _____

PRICE _____ DATE _____

LENGTH/RING SIZE _____ / _____ BUY AGAIN? _____

AFFIX LABEL HERE

FLAVOR WHEEL

- BODY
- DARK FRUIT
- TROPICAL FRUIT
- HERBAL
- SPICY
- SWEET
- VANILLA
- TOFFEE
- CHOCOLATE
- NUTTY
- WOODY
- EARTHY
- LEATHER
- BITTER
- OILY
- LINGER/FINISH

RATING

☆ ☆ ☆ ☆ ☆

FLAVOR STRENGTH

- FULL
- MED. FULL
- MEDIUM
- MILD
- MELLOW

NOTES

_____

_____

_____

_____

_____

NAME OF CIGAR _____

BRAND _____ ORIGIN _____

PRICE _____ DATE _____

LENGTH/RING SIZE _____ / _____ BUY AGAIN? _____

```
AFFIX LABEL HERE
```

FLAVOR WHEEL

- BODY
- DARK FRUIT
- TROPICAL FRUIT
- HERBAL
- SPICY
- SWEET
- VANILLA
- TOFFEE
- CHOCOLATE
- NUTTY
- WOODY
- EARTHY
- LEATHER
- BITTER
- OILY
- LINGER/FINISH

RATING

☆ ☆ ☆ ☆ ☆

FLAVOR STRENGTH

- FULL
- MED. FULL
- MEDIUM
- MILD
- MELLOW

NOTES

_____

_____

_____

_____

_____

NAME OF CIGAR _____

BRAND _____ ORIGIN _____

PRICE _____ DATE _____

LENGTH/RING SIZE _____ / _____ BUY AGAIN? _____

AFFIX LABEL HERE

FLAVOR WHEEL

- BODY
- DARK FRUIT
- TROPICAL FRUIT
- HERBAL
- SPICY
- SWEET
- VANILLA
- TOFFEE
- CHOCOLATE
- NUTTY
- WOODY
- EARTHY
- LEATHER
- BITTER
- OILY
- LINGER/FINISH

RATING

☆☆☆☆☆

FLAVOR STRENGTH

- FULL
- MED. FULL
- MEDIUM
- MILD
- MELLOW

NOTES

_____

_____

_____

_____

_____

NAME OF CIGAR _____

BRAND _____ ORIGIN _____

PRICE _____ DATE _____

LENGTH/RING SIZE _____ / _____ BUY AGAIN? _____

AFFIX LABEL HERE

FLAVOR WHEEL

- BODY
- LINGER/FINISH
- DARK FRUIT
- OILY
- TROPICAL FRUIT
- BITTER
- HERBAL
- LEATHER
- SPICY
- EARTHY
- SWEET
- WOODY
- VANILLA
- NUTTY
- TOFFEE
- CHOCOLATE

RATING

☆☆☆☆☆

FLAVOR STRENGTH

- FULL
- MED. FULL
- MEDIUM
- MILD
- MELLOW

NOTES

_____

_____

_____

_____

_____

NAME OF CIGAR _____

BRAND _____ ORIGIN _____

PRICE _____ DATE _____

LENGTH/RING SIZE _____/_____ BUY AGAIN? _____

AFFIX LABEL HERE

FLAVOR WHEEL

- BODY
- DARK FRUIT
- TROPICAL FRUIT
- HERBAL
- SPICY
- SWEET
- VANILLA
- TOFFEE
- CHOCOLATE
- NUTTY
- WOODY
- EARTHY
- LEATHER
- BITTER
- OILY
- LINGER/FINISH

RATING

☆☆☆☆☆

FLAVOR STRENGTH

- FULL
- MED. FULL
- MEDIUM
- MILD
- MELLOW

NOTES

_____

_____

_____

_____

_____

NAME OF CIGAR _____

BRAND _____ ORIGIN _____

PRICE _____ DATE _____

LENGTH/RING SIZE _____ / _____ BUY AGAIN? _____

```
AFFIX LABEL HERE
```

FLAVOR WHEEL

- BODY
- DARK FRUIT
- TROPICAL FRUIT
- HERBAL
- SPICY
- SWEET
- VANILLA
- TOFFEE
- CHOCOLATE
- NUTTY
- WOODY
- EARTHY
- LEATHER
- BITTER
- OILY
- LINGER/FINISH

RATING

☆ ☆ ☆ ☆ ☆

FLAVOR STRENGTH

- FULL
- MED. FULL
- MEDIUM
- MILD
- MELLOW

NOTES

_____

_____

_____

_____

_____

NAME OF CIGAR _____

BRAND _____ ORIGIN _____

PRICE _____ DATE _____

LENGTH/RING SIZE _____/_____ BUY AGAIN? _____

AFFIX LABEL HERE

FLAVOR WHEEL

- BODY
- DARK FRUIT
- TROPICAL FRUIT
- HERBAL
- SPICY
- SWEET
- VANILLA
- TOFFEE
- CHOCOLATE
- NUTTY
- WOODY
- EARTHY
- LEATHER
- BITTER
- OILY
- LINGER/FINISH

RATING

☆ ☆ ☆ ☆ ☆

FLAVOR STRENGTH

- FULL
- MED. FULL
- MEDIUM
- MILD
- MELLOW

NOTES

_____

_____

_____

_____

_____

NAME OF CIGAR _____

BRAND _____ ORIGIN _____

PRICE _____ DATE _____

LENGTH/RING SIZE _____ / _____ BUY AGAIN? _____

AFFIX LABEL HERE

FLAVOR WHEEL

- BODY
- DARK FRUIT
- TROPICAL FRUIT
- HERBAL
- SPICY
- SWEET
- VANILLA
- TOFFEE
- CHOCOLATE
- NUTTY
- WOODY
- EARTHY
- LEATHER
- BITTER
- OILY
- LINGER/FINISH

RATING

☆☆☆☆☆

FLAVOR STRENGTH

- FULL
- MED. FULL
- MEDIUM
- MILD
- MELLOW

NOTES

_____

_____

_____

_____

_____

NAME OF CIGAR _____

BRAND _____ ORIGIN _____

PRICE _____ DATE _____

LENGTH/RING SIZE _____ / _____ BUY AGAIN? _____

AFFIX LABEL HERE

FLAVOR WHEEL

- BODY
- DARK FRUIT
- TROPICAL FRUIT
- HERBAL
- SPICY
- SWEET
- VANILLA
- TOFFEE
- CHOCOLATE
- NUTTY
- WOODY
- EARTHY
- LEATHER
- BITTER
- OILY
- LINGER/FINISH

RATING

☆☆☆☆☆

FLAVOR STRENGTH

- FULL
- MED. FULL
- MEDIUM
- MILD
- MELLOW

NOTES

_____
_____
_____
_____
_____

NAME OF CIGAR _____

BRAND _____ ORIGIN _____

PRICE _____ DATE _____

LENGTH/RING SIZE _____ / _____ BUY AGAIN? _____

AFFIX LABEL HERE

FLAVOR WHEEL

- BODY
- DARK FRUIT
- TROPICAL FRUIT
- HERBAL
- SPICY
- SWEET
- VANILLA
- TOFFEE
- CHOCOLATE
- NUTTY
- WOODY
- EARTHY
- LEATHER
- BITTER
- OILY
- LINGER/FINISH

RATING

☆ ☆ ☆ ☆ ☆

FLAVOR STRENGTH

- FULL
- MED. FULL
- MEDIUM
- MILD
- MELLOW

NOTES

_____

_____

_____

_____

NAME OF CIGAR _____

BRAND _____ ORIGIN _____

PRICE _____ DATE _____

LENGTH/RING SIZE _____ / _____ BUY AGAIN? _____

AFFIX LABEL HERE

FLAVOR WHEEL

- BODY
- LINGER/FINISH
- OILY
- BITTER
- LEATHER
- EARTHY
- WOODY
- NUTTY
- CHOCOLATE
- TOFFEE
- VANILLA
- SWEET
- SPICY
- HERBAL
- TROPICAL FRUIT
- DARK FRUIT

RATING

☆☆☆☆☆

FLAVOR STRENGTH

- FULL
- MED. FULL
- MEDIUM
- MILD
- MELLOW

NOTES

_____

_____

_____

_____

_____

NAME OF CIGAR _____

BRAND _____ ORIGIN _____

PRICE _____ DATE _____

LENGTH/RING SIZE _____ / _____ BUY AGAIN? _____

AFFIX LABEL HERE

FLAVOR WHEEL

- BODY
- LINGER/FINISH
- DARK FRUIT
- OILY
- TROPICAL FRUIT
- BITTER
- HERBAL
- LEATHER
- SPICY
- EARTHY
- SWEET
- WOODY
- VANILLA
- NUTTY
- TOFFEE
- CHOCOLATE

RATING

☆☆☆☆☆

FLAVOR STRENGTH

- FULL
- MED. FULL
- MEDIUM
- MILD
- MELLOW

NOTES

_____

_____

_____

_____

_____

NAME OF CIGAR _____

BRAND _____ ORIGIN _____

PRICE _____ DATE _____

LENGTH/RING SIZE _____ / _____ BUY AGAIN? _____

AFFIX LABEL HERE

FLAVOR WHEEL

- BODY
- LINGER/FINISH
- DARK FRUIT
- OILY
- TROPICAL FRUIT
- BITTER
- HERBAL
- LEATHER
- SPICY
- EARTHY
- SWEET
- WOODY
- VANILLA
- NUTTY
- TOFFEE
- CHOCOLATE

RATING

☆ ☆ ☆ ☆ ☆

FLAVOR STRENGTH

- FULL
- MED. FULL
- MEDIUM
- MILD
- MELLOW

NOTES

_____

_____

_____

_____

NAME OF CIGAR _____

BRAND _____ ORIGIN _____

PRICE _____ DATE _____

LENGTH/RING SIZE _____/_____ BUY AGAIN? _____

```
AFFIX LABEL HERE
```

FLAVOR WHEEL

- BODY
- DARK FRUIT
- TROPICAL FRUIT
- HERBAL
- SPICY
- SWEET
- VANILLA
- TOFFEE
- CHOCOLATE
- NUTTY
- WOODY
- EARTHY
- LEATHER
- BITTER
- OILY
- LINGER/FINISH

RATING

☆☆☆☆☆

FLAVOR STRENGTH

- FULL
- MED. FULL
- MEDIUM
- MILD
- MELLOW

NOTES

_____
_____
_____
_____
_____

NAME OF CIGAR ____________________

BRAND ____________________ ORIGIN ____________________

PRICE ____________________ DATE ____________________

LENGTH/RING SIZE ________/________ BUY AGAIN? ____________________

AFFIX LABEL HERE

FLAVOR WHEEL

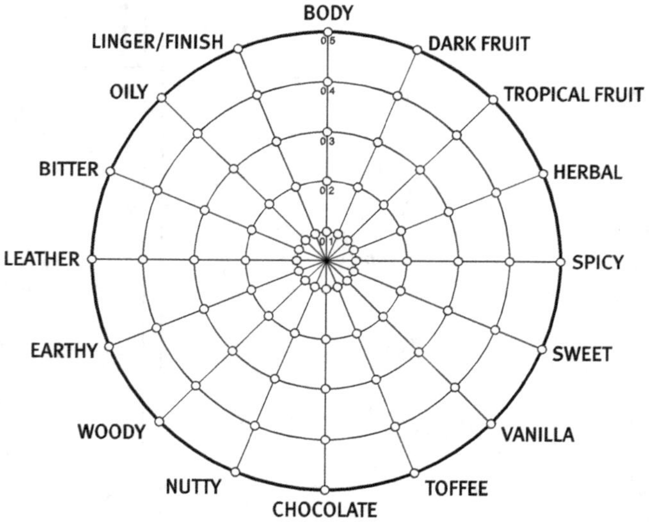
BODY
DARK FRUIT
TROPICAL FRUIT
HERBAL
SPICY
SWEET
VANILLA
TOFFEE
CHOCOLATE
NUTTY
WOODY
EARTHY
LEATHER
BITTER
OILY
LINGER/FINISH

RATING

☆☆☆☆☆

FLAVOR STRENGTH

FULL
MED. FULL
MEDIUM
MILD
MELLOW

NOTES

____

____

____

____

____

NAME OF CIGAR _____

BRAND _____ ORIGIN _____

PRICE _____ DATE _____

LENGTH/RING SIZE _____ / _____ BUY AGAIN? _____

AFFIX LABEL HERE

FLAVOR WHEEL

- BODY
- LINGER/FINISH
- OILY
- BITTER
- LEATHER
- EARTHY
- WOODY
- NUTTY
- CHOCOLATE
- TOFFEE
- VANILLA
- SWEET
- SPICY
- HERBAL
- TROPICAL FRUIT
- DARK FRUIT

RATING

☆ ☆ ☆ ☆ ☆

FLAVOR STRENGTH

- FULL
- MED. FULL
- MEDIUM
- MILD
- MELLOW

NOTES

_____

_____

_____

_____

_____

NAME OF CIGAR _____

BRAND _____ ORIGIN _____

PRICE _____ DATE _____

LENGTH/RING SIZE _____ / _____ BUY AGAIN? _____

AFFIX LABEL HERE

FLAVOR WHEEL

- BODY
- DARK FRUIT
- TROPICAL FRUIT
- HERBAL
- SPICY
- SWEET
- VANILLA
- TOFFEE
- CHOCOLATE
- NUTTY
- WOODY
- EARTHY
- LEATHER
- BITTER
- OILY
- LINGER/FINISH

(scale 0.1 – 0.5)

RATING

☆ ☆ ☆ ☆ ☆

FLAVOR STRENGTH

- FULL
- MED. FULL
- MEDIUM
- MILD
- MELLOW

NOTES

_____
_____
_____
_____
_____

NAME OF CIGAR _____

BRAND _____ ORIGIN _____

PRICE _____ DATE _____

LENGTH/RING SIZE _____ / _____ BUY AGAIN? _____

AFFIX LABEL HERE

FLAVOR WHEEL

- BODY
- DARK FRUIT
- TROPICAL FRUIT
- HERBAL
- SPICY
- SWEET
- VANILLA
- TOFFEE
- CHOCOLATE
- NUTTY
- WOODY
- EARTHY
- LEATHER
- BITTER
- OILY
- LINGER/FINISH

RATING

☆☆☆☆☆

FLAVOR STRENGTH

- FULL
- MED. FULL
- MEDIUM
- MILD
- MELLOW

NOTES

_____

_____

_____

_____

_____

NAME OF CIGAR _____

BRAND _____ ORIGIN _____

PRICE _____ DATE _____

LENGTH/RING SIZE _____ / _____ BUY AGAIN? _____

AFFIX LABEL HERE

FLAVOR WHEEL

- BODY
- DARK FRUIT
- TROPICAL FRUIT
- HERBAL
- SPICY
- SWEET
- VANILLA
- TOFFEE
- CHOCOLATE
- NUTTY
- WOODY
- EARTHY
- LEATHER
- BITTER
- OILY
- LINGER/FINISH

RATING

☆☆☆☆☆

FLAVOR STRENGTH

- FULL
- MED. FULL
- MEDIUM
- MILD
- MELLOW

NOTES

_____
_____
_____
_____
_____

NAME OF CIGAR _____

BRAND _____ ORIGIN _____

PRICE _____ DATE _____

LENGTH/RING SIZE _____ / _____ BUY AGAIN? _____

AFFIX LABEL HERE

FLAVOR WHEEL

- BODY
- DARK FRUIT
- TROPICAL FRUIT
- HERBAL
- SPICY
- SWEET
- VANILLA
- TOFFEE
- CHOCOLATE
- NUTTY
- WOODY
- EARTHY
- LEATHER
- BITTER
- OILY
- LINGER/FINISH

RATING
☆ ☆ ☆ ☆ ☆

FLAVOR STRENGTH
- FULL
- MED. FULL
- MEDIUM
- MILD
- MELLOW

NOTES
_____
_____
_____
_____
_____

NAME OF CIGAR _____

BRAND _____ ORIGIN _____

PRICE _____ DATE _____

LENGTH/RING SIZE _____ / _____ BUY AGAIN? _____

```
AFFIX LABEL HERE
```

FLAVOR WHEEL

- BODY
- LINGER/FINISH
- OILY
- BITTER
- LEATHER
- EARTHY
- WOODY
- NUTTY
- CHOCOLATE
- TOFFEE
- VANILLA
- SWEET
- SPICY
- HERBAL
- TROPICAL FRUIT
- DARK FRUIT

RATING

☆ ☆ ☆ ☆ ☆

FLAVOR STRENGTH

- FULL
- MED. FULL
- MEDIUM
- MILD
- MELLOW

NOTES

_____

_____

_____

_____

_____

NAME OF CIGAR _____

BRAND _____ ORIGIN _____

PRICE _____ DATE _____

LENGTH/RING SIZE _____ / _____ BUY AGAIN? _____

AFFIX LABEL HERE

FLAVOR WHEEL

- BODY
- DARK FRUIT
- TROPICAL FRUIT
- HERBAL
- SPICY
- SWEET
- VANILLA
- TOFFEE
- CHOCOLATE
- NUTTY
- WOODY
- EARTHY
- LEATHER
- BITTER
- OILY
- LINGER/FINISH

RATING

☆ ☆ ☆ ☆ ☆

FLAVOR STRENGTH

- FULL
- MED. FULL
- MEDIUM
- MILD
- MELLOW

NOTES

_____

_____

_____

_____

_____

NAME OF CIGAR _____

BRAND _____ ORIGIN _____

PRICE _____ DATE _____

LENGTH/RING SIZE _____ / _____ BUY AGAIN? _____

AFFIX LABEL HERE

FLAVOR WHEEL

- BODY
- DARK FRUIT
- TROPICAL FRUIT
- HERBAL
- SPICY
- SWEET
- VANILLA
- TOFFEE
- CHOCOLATE
- NUTTY
- WOODY
- EARTHY
- LEATHER
- BITTER
- OILY
- LINGER/FINISH

RATING

☆ ☆ ☆ ☆ ☆

FLAVOR STRENGTH

- FULL
- MED. FULL
- MEDIUM
- MILD
- MELLOW

NOTES

_____
_____
_____
_____
_____

NAME OF CIGAR _____

BRAND _____ ORIGIN _____

PRICE _____ DATE _____

LENGTH/RING SIZE _____ / _____ BUY AGAIN? _____

```
AFFIX LABEL HERE
```

FLAVOR WHEEL

- BODY
- LINGER/FINISH
- OILY
- BITTER
- LEATHER
- EARTHY
- WOODY
- NUTTY
- CHOCOLATE
- TOFFEE
- VANILLA
- SWEET
- SPICY
- HERBAL
- TROPICAL FRUIT
- DARK FRUIT

RATING

☆☆☆☆☆

FLAVOR STRENGTH

- FULL
- MED. FULL
- MEDIUM
- MILD
- MELLOW

NOTES

_____

_____

_____

_____

_____

NAME OF CIGAR _____

BRAND _____ ORIGIN _____

PRICE _____ DATE _____

LENGTH/RING SIZE _____ / _____ BUY AGAIN? _____

AFFIX LABEL HERE

FLAVOR WHEEL

- BODY
- LINGER/FINISH
- DARK FRUIT
- OILY
- TROPICAL FRUIT
- BITTER
- HERBAL
- LEATHER
- SPICY
- EARTHY
- SWEET
- WOODY
- VANILLA
- NUTTY
- TOFFEE
- CHOCOLATE

RATING

☆☆☆☆☆

FLAVOR STRENGTH

- FULL
- MED. FULL
- MEDIUM
- MILD
- MELLOW

NOTES

_____

_____

_____

_____

_____

NAME OF CIGAR _____

BRAND _____ ORIGIN _____

PRICE _____ DATE _____

LENGTH/RING SIZE _____ / _____ BUY AGAIN? _____

AFFIX LABEL HERE

FLAVOR WHEEL

- BODY
- DARK FRUIT
- TROPICAL FRUIT
- HERBAL
- SPICY
- SWEET
- VANILLA
- TOFFEE
- CHOCOLATE
- NUTTY
- WOODY
- EARTHY
- LEATHER
- BITTER
- OILY
- LINGER/FINISH

RATING

☆ ☆ ☆ ☆ ☆

FLAVOR STRENGTH

- FULL
- MED. FULL
- MEDIUM
- MILD
- MELLOW

NOTES

_____

_____

_____

_____

_____

NAME OF CIGAR _____

BRAND _____ ORIGIN _____

PRICE _____ DATE _____

LENGTH/RING SIZE _____ / _____ BUY AGAIN? _____

AFFIX LABEL HERE

FLAVOR WHEEL

Flavor wheel with axes: BODY, DARK FRUIT, TROPICAL FRUIT, HERBAL, SPICY, SWEET, VANILLA, TOFFEE, CHOCOLATE, NUTTY, WOODY, EARTHY, LEATHER, BITTER, OILY, LINGER/FINISH (scale 0–5)

RATING

☆ ☆ ☆ ☆ ☆

FLAVOR STRENGTH

- FULL
- MED. FULL
- MEDIUM
- MILD
- MELLOW

NOTES

_____

_____

_____

_____

_____

NAME OF CIGAR _____

BRAND _____ ORIGIN _____

PRICE _____ DATE _____

LENGTH/RING SIZE _____ / _____ BUY AGAIN? _____

AFFIX LABEL HERE

FLAVOR WHEEL

- BODY
- DARK FRUIT
- TROPICAL FRUIT
- HERBAL
- SPICY
- SWEET
- VANILLA
- TOFFEE
- CHOCOLATE
- NUTTY
- WOODY
- EARTHY
- LEATHER
- BITTER
- OILY
- LINGER/FINISH

RATING

☆ ☆ ☆ ☆ ☆

FLAVOR STRENGTH

- FULL
- MED. FULL
- MEDIUM
- MILD
- MELLOW

NOTES

_____

_____

_____

_____

_____

NAME OF CIGAR _____

BRAND _____ ORIGIN _____

PRICE _____ DATE _____

LENGTH/RING SIZE _____/_____ BUY AGAIN? _____

AFFIX LABEL HERE

FLAVOR WHEEL

- BODY
- DARK FRUIT
- TROPICAL FRUIT
- HERBAL
- SPICY
- SWEET
- VANILLA
- TOFFEE
- CHOCOLATE
- NUTTY
- WOODY
- EARTHY
- LEATHER
- BITTER
- OILY
- LINGER/FINISH

RATING

☆ ☆ ☆ ☆ ☆

FLAVOR STRENGTH

- FULL
- MED. FULL
- MEDIUM
- MILD
- MELLOW

NOTES

_____
_____
_____
_____
_____

NAME OF CIGAR _____

BRAND _____ ORIGIN _____

PRICE _____ DATE _____

LENGTH/RING SIZE _____ / _____ BUY AGAIN? _____

AFFIX LABEL HERE

FLAVOR WHEEL

- BODY
- DARK FRUIT
- TROPICAL FRUIT
- HERBAL
- SPICY
- SWEET
- VANILLA
- TOFFEE
- CHOCOLATE
- NUTTY
- WOODY
- EARTHY
- LEATHER
- BITTER
- OILY
- LINGER/FINISH

RATING

☆ ☆ ☆ ☆ ☆

FLAVOR STRENGTH

- FULL
- MED. FULL
- MEDIUM
- MILD
- MELLOW

NOTES

_____

_____

_____

_____

_____

NAME OF CIGAR _____

BRAND _____ ORIGIN _____

PRICE _____ DATE _____

LENGTH/RING SIZE _____ / _____ BUY AGAIN? _____

AFFIX LABEL HERE

FLAVOR WHEEL

- BODY
- DARK FRUIT
- TROPICAL FRUIT
- HERBAL
- SPICY
- SWEET
- VANILLA
- TOFFEE
- CHOCOLATE
- NUTTY
- WOODY
- EARTHY
- LEATHER
- BITTER
- OILY
- LINGER/FINISH

RATING

☆☆☆☆☆

FLAVOR STRENGTH

- FULL
- MED. FULL
- MEDIUM
- MILD
- MELLOW

NOTES

_____

_____

_____

_____

_____

NAME OF CIGAR _____

BRAND _____ ORIGIN _____

PRICE _____ DATE _____

LENGTH/RING SIZE _____ / _____ BUY AGAIN? _____

AFFIX LABEL HERE

FLAVOR WHEEL

- BODY
- DARK FRUIT
- TROPICAL FRUIT
- HERBAL
- SPICY
- SWEET
- VANILLA
- TOFFEE
- CHOCOLATE
- NUTTY
- WOODY
- EARTHY
- LEATHER
- BITTER
- OILY
- LINGER/FINISH

RATING

☆ ☆ ☆ ☆ ☆

FLAVOR STRENGTH

- FULL
- MED. FULL
- MEDIUM
- MILD
- MELLOW

NOTES

_____

_____

_____

_____

_____

NAME OF CIGAR _____

BRAND _____ ORIGIN _____

PRICE _____ DATE _____

LENGTH/RING SIZE _____/_____ BUY AGAIN? _____

AFFIX LABEL HERE

FLAVOR WHEEL

- BODY
- DARK FRUIT
- TROPICAL FRUIT
- HERBAL
- SPICY
- SWEET
- VANILLA
- TOFFEE
- CHOCOLATE
- NUTTY
- WOODY
- EARTHY
- LEATHER
- BITTER
- OILY
- LINGER/FINISH

RATING

☆ ☆ ☆ ☆ ☆

FLAVOR STRENGTH

- FULL
- MED. FULL
- MEDIUM
- MILD
- MELLOW

NOTES

_____

_____

_____

_____

_____

NAME OF CIGAR _____

BRAND _____ ORIGIN _____

PRICE _____ DATE _____

LENGTH/RING SIZE _____ / _____ BUY AGAIN? _____

AFFIX LABEL HERE

FLAVOR WHEEL

- BODY
- DARK FRUIT
- TROPICAL FRUIT
- HERBAL
- SPICY
- SWEET
- VANILLA
- TOFFEE
- CHOCOLATE
- NUTTY
- WOODY
- EARTHY
- LEATHER
- BITTER
- OILY
- LINGER/FINISH

RATING

☆ ☆ ☆ ☆ ☆

FLAVOR STRENGTH

- FULL
- MED. FULL
- MEDIUM
- MILD
- MELLOW

NOTES

_____

_____

_____

_____

_____

NAME OF CIGAR _____

BRAND _____ ORIGIN _____

PRICE _____ DATE _____

LENGTH/RING SIZE _____ / _____ BUY AGAIN? _____

AFFIX LABEL HERE

FLAVOR WHEEL

- BODY
- DARK FRUIT
- TROPICAL FRUIT
- HERBAL
- SPICY
- SWEET
- VANILLA
- TOFFEE
- CHOCOLATE
- NUTTY
- WOODY
- EARTHY
- LEATHER
- BITTER
- OILY
- LINGER/FINISH

RATING

☆ ☆ ☆ ☆ ☆

FLAVOR STRENGTH

- FULL
- MED. FULL
- MEDIUM
- MILD
- MELLOW

NOTES

_____

_____

_____

_____

_____

NAME OF CIGAR _____

BRAND _____ ORIGIN _____

PRICE _____ DATE _____

LENGTH/RING SIZE _____ / _____ BUY AGAIN? _____

AFFIX LABEL HERE

FLAVOR WHEEL

- BODY
- LINGER/FINISH
- OILY
- BITTER
- LEATHER
- EARTHY
- WOODY
- NUTTY
- CHOCOLATE
- TOFFEE
- VANILLA
- SWEET
- SPICY
- HERBAL
- TROPICAL FRUIT
- DARK FRUIT

RATING

☆ ☆ ☆ ☆ ☆

FLAVOR STRENGTH

- FULL
- MED. FULL
- MEDIUM
- MILD
- MELLOW

NOTES

_____

_____

_____

_____

_____

NAME OF CIGAR _____

BRAND _____ ORIGIN _____

PRICE _____ DATE _____

LENGTH/RING SIZE _____ / _____ BUY AGAIN? _____

AFFIX LABEL HERE

FLAVOR WHEEL

- BODY
- LINGER/FINISH
- OILY
- BITTER
- LEATHER
- EARTHY
- WOODY
- NUTTY
- CHOCOLATE
- TOFFEE
- VANILLA
- SWEET
- SPICY
- HERBAL
- TROPICAL FRUIT
- DARK FRUIT

RATING

☆☆☆☆☆

FLAVOR STRENGTH

- FULL
- MED. FULL
- MEDIUM
- MILD
- MELLOW

NOTES

_____
_____
_____
_____
_____

NAME OF CIGAR _____

BRAND _____ ORIGIN _____

PRICE _____ DATE _____

LENGTH/RING SIZE _____ / _____ BUY AGAIN? _____

AFFIX LABEL HERE

FLAVOR WHEEL

- BODY
- LINGER/FINISH
- DARK FRUIT
- OILY
- TROPICAL FRUIT
- BITTER
- HERBAL
- LEATHER
- SPICY
- EARTHY
- SWEET
- WOODY
- VANILLA
- NUTTY
- TOFFEE
- CHOCOLATE

RATING

☆ ☆ ☆ ☆ ☆

FLAVOR STRENGTH

- FULL
- MED. FULL
- MEDIUM
- MILD
- MELLOW

NOTES

_____

_____

_____

_____

_____

NAME OF CIGAR _____

BRAND _____ ORIGIN _____

PRICE _____ DATE _____

LENGTH/RING SIZE _____ / _____ BUY AGAIN? _____

AFFIX LABEL HERE

FLAVOR WHEEL

- BODY
- DARK FRUIT
- TROPICAL FRUIT
- HERBAL
- SPICY
- SWEET
- VANILLA
- TOFFEE
- CHOCOLATE
- NUTTY
- WOODY
- EARTHY
- LEATHER
- BITTER
- OILY
- LINGER/FINISH

RATING

☆☆☆☆☆

FLAVOR STRENGTH

- FULL
- MED. FULL
- MEDIUM
- MILD
- MELLOW

NOTES

_____

_____

_____

_____

_____

NAME OF CIGAR _____

BRAND _____ ORIGIN _____

PRICE _____ DATE _____

LENGTH/RING SIZE _____ / _____ BUY AGAIN? _____

```
┌─ ─ ─ ─ ─ ─ ─ ─ ─ ─ ─ ─ ─ ─ ─ ─ ─ ─ ─ ─ ─ ─ ─ ─ ┐
            AFFIX LABEL HERE
└─ ─ ─ ─ ─ ─ ─ ─ ─ ─ ─ ─ ─ ─ ─ ─ ─ ─ ─ ─ ─ ─ ─ ─ ┘
```

FLAVOR WHEEL

Categories: BODY, DARK FRUIT, TROPICAL FRUIT, HERBAL, SPICY, SWEET, VANILLA, TOFFEE, CHOCOLATE, NUTTY, WOODY, EARTHY, LEATHER, BITTER, OILY, LINGER/FINISH

RATING

☆ ☆ ☆ ☆ ☆

FLAVOR STRENGTH

- FULL
- MED. FULL
- MEDIUM
- MILD
- MELLOW

NOTES

_____
_____
_____
_____
_____

NAME OF CIGAR _____

BRAND _____ ORIGIN _____

PRICE _____ DATE _____

LENGTH/RING SIZE _____ / _____ BUY AGAIN? _____

AFFIX LABEL HERE

FLAVOR WHEEL

- BODY
- LINGER/FINISH
- OILY
- BITTER
- LEATHER
- EARTHY
- WOODY
- NUTTY
- CHOCOLATE
- TOFFEE
- VANILLA
- SWEET
- SPICY
- HERBAL
- TROPICAL FRUIT
- DARK FRUIT

RATING

☆ ☆ ☆ ☆ ☆

FLAVOR STRENGTH

- FULL
- MED. FULL
- MEDIUM
- MILD
- MELLOW

NOTES

_____
_____
_____
_____
_____

NAME OF CIGAR _____

BRAND _____ ORIGIN _____

PRICE _____ DATE _____

LENGTH/RING SIZE _____ / _____ BUY AGAIN? _____

AFFIX LABEL HERE

FLAVOR WHEEL

- BODY
- DARK FRUIT
- TROPICAL FRUIT
- HERBAL
- SPICY
- SWEET
- VANILLA
- TOFFEE
- CHOCOLATE
- NUTTY
- WOODY
- EARTHY
- LEATHER
- BITTER
- OILY
- LINGER/FINISH

RATING

☆☆☆☆☆

FLAVOR STRENGTH

- FULL
- MED. FULL
- MEDIUM
- MILD
- MELLOW

NOTES

_____

_____

_____

_____

_____

NAME OF CIGAR _____

BRAND _____ ORIGIN _____

PRICE _____ DATE _____

LENGTH/RING SIZE _____ / _____ BUY AGAIN? _____

AFFIX LABEL HERE

FLAVOR WHEEL

- BODY
- DARK FRUIT
- TROPICAL FRUIT
- HERBAL
- SPICY
- SWEET
- VANILLA
- TOFFEE
- CHOCOLATE
- NUTTY
- WOODY
- EARTHY
- LEATHER
- BITTER
- OILY
- LINGER/FINISH

RATING

☆ ☆ ☆ ☆ ☆

FLAVOR STRENGTH

- FULL
- MED. FULL
- MEDIUM
- MILD
- MELLOW

NOTES

_____

_____

_____

_____

_____

NAME OF CIGAR _____

BRAND _____ ORIGIN _____

PRICE _____ DATE _____

LENGTH/RING SIZE _____ / _____ BUY AGAIN? _____

AFFIX LABEL HERE

FLAVOR WHEEL

- BODY
- DARK FRUIT
- TROPICAL FRUIT
- HERBAL
- SPICY
- SWEET
- VANILLA
- TOFFEE
- CHOCOLATE
- NUTTY
- WOODY
- EARTHY
- LEATHER
- BITTER
- OILY
- LINGER/FINISH

RATING

☆ ☆ ☆ ☆ ☆

FLAVOR STRENGTH

- FULL
- MED. FULL
- MEDIUM
- MILD
- MELLOW

NOTES

_____

_____

_____

_____

_____

NAME OF CIGAR ______________________________

BRAND ______________________ ORIGIN ______________________

PRICE ______________________ DATE ______________________

LENGTH/RING SIZE ________/________ BUY AGAIN? ______________________

AFFIX LABEL HERE

FLAVOR WHEEL

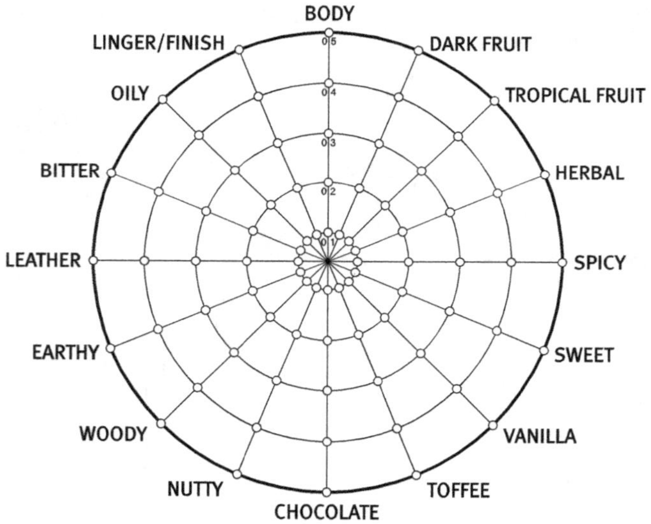
BODY
DARK FRUIT
TROPICAL FRUIT
HERBAL
SPICY
SWEET
VANILLA
TOFFEE
CHOCOLATE
NUTTY
WOODY
EARTHY
LEATHER
BITTER
OILY
LINGER/FINISH

RATING

☆☆☆☆☆

FLAVOR STRENGTH

FULL
MED. FULL
MEDIUM
MILD
MELLOW

NOTES

____

____

____

____

____

NAME OF CIGAR _____

BRAND _____ ORIGIN _____

PRICE _____ DATE _____

LENGTH/RING SIZE _____ / _____ BUY AGAIN? _____

```
AFFIX LABEL HERE
```

FLAVOR WHEEL

- BODY
- LINGER/FINISH
- OILY
- BITTER
- LEATHER
- EARTHY
- WOODY
- NUTTY
- CHOCOLATE
- TOFFEE
- VANILLA
- SWEET
- SPICY
- HERBAL
- TROPICAL FRUIT
- DARK FRUIT

RATING
☆☆☆☆☆

FLAVOR STRENGTH
- FULL
- MED. FULL
- MEDIUM
- MILD
- MELLOW

NOTES

_____

_____

_____

_____

_____

NAME OF CIGAR _____

BRAND _____ ORIGIN _____

PRICE _____ DATE _____

LENGTH/RING SIZE _____ / _____ BUY AGAIN? _____

AFFIX LABEL HERE

FLAVOR WHEEL

- BODY
- DARK FRUIT
- TROPICAL FRUIT
- HERBAL
- SPICY
- SWEET
- VANILLA
- TOFFEE
- CHOCOLATE
- NUTTY
- WOODY
- EARTHY
- LEATHER
- BITTER
- OILY
- LINGER/FINISH

RATING

☆☆☆☆☆

FLAVOR STRENGTH

- FULL
- MED. FULL
- MEDIUM
- MILD
- MELLOW

NOTES

_____
_____
_____
_____
_____

NAME OF CIGAR _____

BRAND _____ ORIGIN _____

PRICE _____ DATE _____

LENGTH/RING SIZE _____ / _____ BUY AGAIN? _____

AFFIX LABEL HERE

FLAVOR WHEEL

- BODY
- LINGER/FINISH
- DARK FRUIT
- OILY
- TROPICAL FRUIT
- BITTER
- HERBAL
- LEATHER
- SPICY
- EARTHY
- SWEET
- WOODY
- VANILLA
- NUTTY
- TOFFEE
- CHOCOLATE

RATING

☆ ☆ ☆ ☆ ☆

FLAVOR STRENGTH

- FULL
- MED. FULL
- MEDIUM
- MILD
- MELLOW

NOTES

_____

_____

_____

_____

_____

NAME OF CIGAR _____

BRAND _____ ORIGIN _____

PRICE _____ DATE _____

LENGTH/RING SIZE _____ / _____ BUY AGAIN? _____

AFFIX LABEL HERE

FLAVOR WHEEL

- BODY
- DARK FRUIT
- TROPICAL FRUIT
- HERBAL
- SPICY
- SWEET
- VANILLA
- TOFFEE
- CHOCOLATE
- NUTTY
- WOODY
- EARTHY
- LEATHER
- BITTER
- OILY
- LINGER/FINISH

RATING

☆ ☆ ☆ ☆ ☆

FLAVOR STRENGTH

- FULL
- MED. FULL
- MEDIUM
- MILD
- MELLOW

NOTES

_____

_____

_____

_____

NAME OF CIGAR _____

BRAND _____ ORIGIN _____

PRICE _____ DATE _____

LENGTH/RING SIZE _____ / _____ BUY AGAIN? _____

AFFIX LABEL HERE

FLAVOR WHEEL

- BODY
- DARK FRUIT
- TROPICAL FRUIT
- HERBAL
- SPICY
- SWEET
- VANILLA
- TOFFEE
- CHOCOLATE
- NUTTY
- WOODY
- EARTHY
- LEATHER
- BITTER
- OILY
- LINGER/FINISH

RATING
☆☆☆☆☆

FLAVOR STRENGTH
- FULL
- MED. FULL
- MEDIUM
- MILD
- MELLOW

NOTES

_____

_____

_____

_____

_____

NAME OF CIGAR _____

BRAND _____ ORIGIN _____

PRICE _____ DATE _____

LENGTH/RING SIZE _____ / _____ BUY AGAIN? _____

AFFIX LABEL HERE

FLAVOR WHEEL

- BODY
- DARK FRUIT
- TROPICAL FRUIT
- HERBAL
- SPICY
- SWEET
- VANILLA
- TOFFEE
- CHOCOLATE
- NUTTY
- WOODY
- EARTHY
- LEATHER
- BITTER
- OILY
- LINGER/FINISH

RATING

☆ ☆ ☆ ☆ ☆

FLAVOR STRENGTH

- FULL
- MED. FULL
- MEDIUM
- MILD
- MELLOW

NOTES

_____

_____

_____

_____

_____

NAME OF CIGAR _____

BRAND _____ ORIGIN _____

PRICE _____ DATE _____

LENGTH/RING SIZE _____ / _____ BUY AGAIN? _____

AFFIX LABEL HERE

FLAVOR WHEEL

- BODY
- LINGER/FINISH
- OILY
- BITTER
- LEATHER
- EARTHY
- WOODY
- NUTTY
- CHOCOLATE
- TOFFEE
- VANILLA
- SWEET
- SPICY
- HERBAL
- TROPICAL FRUIT
- DARK FRUIT

RATING

☆☆☆☆☆

FLAVOR STRENGTH

- FULL
- MED. FULL
- MEDIUM
- MILD
- MELLOW

NOTES

_____
_____
_____
_____
_____

NAME OF CIGAR _____

BRAND _____ ORIGIN _____

PRICE _____ DATE _____

LENGTH/RING SIZE _____ / _____ BUY AGAIN? _____

AFFIX LABEL HERE

FLAVOR WHEEL

- BODY
- DARK FRUIT
- TROPICAL FRUIT
- HERBAL
- SPICY
- SWEET
- VANILLA
- TOFFEE
- CHOCOLATE
- NUTTY
- WOODY
- EARTHY
- LEATHER
- BITTER
- OILY
- LINGER/FINISH

RATING
☆ ☆ ☆ ☆ ☆

FLAVOR STRENGTH
- FULL
- MED. FULL
- MEDIUM
- MILD
- MELLOW

NOTES
_____
_____
_____
_____
_____

NAME OF CIGAR _____

BRAND _____ ORIGIN _____

PRICE _____ DATE _____

LENGTH/RING SIZE _____ / _____ BUY AGAIN? _____

```
╔═══════════════════════════════════════╗
║           AFFIX LABEL HERE            ║
╚═══════════════════════════════════════╝
```

FLAVOR WHEEL

- BODY
- DARK FRUIT
- TROPICAL FRUIT
- HERBAL
- SPICY
- SWEET
- VANILLA
- TOFFEE
- CHOCOLATE
- NUTTY
- WOODY
- EARTHY
- LEATHER
- BITTER
- OILY
- LINGER/FINISH

RATING

☆ ☆ ☆ ☆ ☆

FLAVOR STRENGTH

- FULL
- MED. FULL
- MEDIUM
- MILD
- MELLOW

NOTES

_____

_____

_____

_____

NAME OF CIGAR _____

BRAND _____ ORIGIN _____

PRICE _____ DATE _____

LENGTH/RING SIZE _____ / _____ BUY AGAIN? _____

AFFIX LABEL HERE

FLAVOR WHEEL

- BODY
- DARK FRUIT
- TROPICAL FRUIT
- HERBAL
- SPICY
- SWEET
- VANILLA
- TOFFEE
- CHOCOLATE
- NUTTY
- WOODY
- EARTHY
- LEATHER
- BITTER
- OILY
- LINGER/FINISH

RATING

☆ ☆ ☆ ☆ ☆

FLAVOR STRENGTH

- FULL
- MED. FULL
- MEDIUM
- MILD
- MELLOW

NOTES

_____

_____

_____

_____

_____

NAME OF CIGAR _____

BRAND _____ ORIGIN _____

PRICE _____ DATE _____

LENGTH/RING SIZE _____ / _____ BUY AGAIN? _____

AFFIX LABEL HERE

FLAVOR WHEEL

- BODY
- LINGER/FINISH
- OILY
- BITTER
- LEATHER
- EARTHY
- WOODY
- NUTTY
- CHOCOLATE
- TOFFEE
- VANILLA
- SWEET
- SPICY
- HERBAL
- TROPICAL FRUIT
- DARK FRUIT

RATING

☆☆☆☆☆

FLAVOR STRENGTH

- FULL
- MED. FULL
- MEDIUM
- MILD
- MELLOW

NOTES

_____
_____
_____
_____
_____

NAME OF CIGAR _____

BRAND _____ ORIGIN _____

PRICE _____ DATE _____

LENGTH/RING SIZE _____/_____ BUY AGAIN? _____

AFFIX LABEL HERE

FLAVOR WHEEL

- BODY
- DARK FRUIT
- TROPICAL FRUIT
- HERBAL
- SPICY
- SWEET
- VANILLA
- TOFFEE
- CHOCOLATE
- NUTTY
- WOODY
- EARTHY
- LEATHER
- BITTER
- OILY
- LINGER/FINISH

RATING

☆☆☆☆☆

FLAVOR STRENGTH

- FULL
- MED. FULL
- MEDIUM
- MILD
- MELLOW

NOTES

_____
_____
_____
_____
_____

NAME OF CIGAR _____

BRAND _____ ORIGIN _____

PRICE _____ DATE _____

LENGTH/RING SIZE _____ / _____ BUY AGAIN? _____

AFFIX LABEL HERE

FLAVOR WHEEL

- BODY
- DARK FRUIT
- TROPICAL FRUIT
- HERBAL
- SPICY
- SWEET
- VANILLA
- TOFFEE
- CHOCOLATE
- NUTTY
- WOODY
- EARTHY
- LEATHER
- BITTER
- OILY
- LINGER/FINISH

RATING

☆☆☆☆☆

FLAVOR STRENGTH

- FULL
- MED. FULL
- MEDIUM
- MILD
- MELLOW

NOTES

_____

_____

_____

_____

_____

NAME OF CIGAR _____

BRAND _____ ORIGIN _____

PRICE _____ DATE _____

LENGTH/RING SIZE _____ / _____ BUY AGAIN? _____

AFFIX LABEL HERE

FLAVOR WHEEL

- BODY
- DARK FRUIT
- TROPICAL FRUIT
- HERBAL
- SPICY
- SWEET
- VANILLA
- TOFFEE
- CHOCOLATE
- NUTTY
- WOODY
- EARTHY
- LEATHER
- BITTER
- OILY
- LINGER/FINISH

RATING

☆ ☆ ☆ ☆ ☆

FLAVOR STRENGTH

- FULL
- MED. FULL
- MEDIUM
- MILD
- MELLOW

NOTES

_____

_____

_____

_____

_____

NAME OF CIGAR _____

BRAND _____ ORIGIN _____

PRICE _____ DATE _____

LENGTH/RING SIZE _____ / _____ BUY AGAIN? _____

AFFIX LABEL HERE

FLAVOR WHEEL

- BODY
- DARK FRUIT
- TROPICAL FRUIT
- HERBAL
- SPICY
- SWEET
- VANILLA
- TOFFEE
- CHOCOLATE
- NUTTY
- WOODY
- EARTHY
- LEATHER
- BITTER
- OILY
- LINGER/FINISH

RATING

☆ ☆ ☆ ☆ ☆

FLAVOR STRENGTH

- FULL
- MED. FULL
- MEDIUM
- MILD
- MELLOW

NOTES

_____
_____
_____
_____
_____

NAME OF CIGAR _____

BRAND _____ ORIGIN _____

PRICE _____ DATE _____

LENGTH/RING SIZE _____ / _____ BUY AGAIN? _____

AFFIX LABEL HERE

FLAVOR WHEEL

- BODY
- LINGER/FINISH
- DARK FRUIT
- OILY
- TROPICAL FRUIT
- BITTER
- HERBAL
- LEATHER
- SPICY
- EARTHY
- SWEET
- WOODY
- VANILLA
- NUTTY
- TOFFEE
- CHOCOLATE

RATING

☆ ☆ ☆ ☆ ☆

FLAVOR STRENGTH

- FULL
- MED. FULL
- MEDIUM
- MILD
- MELLOW

NOTES

_____

_____

_____

_____

_____

NAME OF CIGAR _____

BRAND _____ ORIGIN _____

PRICE _____ DATE _____

LENGTH/RING SIZE _____ / _____ BUY AGAIN? _____

AFFIX LABEL HERE

FLAVOR WHEEL

- BODY
- LINGER/FINISH
- DARK FRUIT
- OILY
- TROPICAL FRUIT
- BITTER
- HERBAL
- LEATHER
- SPICY
- EARTHY
- SWEET
- WOODY
- VANILLA
- NUTTY
- TOFFEE
- CHOCOLATE

RATING
☆☆☆☆☆

FLAVOR STRENGTH
- FULL
- MED. FULL
- MEDIUM
- MILD
- MELLOW

NOTES

_____

_____

_____

_____

NAME OF CIGAR _____

BRAND _____ ORIGIN _____

PRICE _____ DATE _____

LENGTH/RING SIZE _____/_____ BUY AGAIN? _____

AFFIX LABEL HERE

FLAVOR WHEEL

- BODY
- DARK FRUIT
- TROPICAL FRUIT
- HERBAL
- SPICY
- SWEET
- VANILLA
- TOFFEE
- CHOCOLATE
- NUTTY
- WOODY
- EARTHY
- LEATHER
- BITTER
- OILY
- LINGER/FINISH

RATING

☆☆☆☆☆

FLAVOR STRENGTH

- FULL
- MED. FULL
- MEDIUM
- MILD
- MELLOW

NOTES

_____
_____
_____
_____
_____

NAME OF CIGAR _____

BRAND _____ ORIGIN _____

PRICE _____ DATE _____

LENGTH/RING SIZE _____ / _____ BUY AGAIN? _____

AFFIX LABEL HERE

FLAVOR WHEEL

- BODY
- DARK FRUIT
- TROPICAL FRUIT
- HERBAL
- SPICY
- SWEET
- VANILLA
- TOFFEE
- CHOCOLATE
- NUTTY
- WOODY
- EARTHY
- LEATHER
- BITTER
- OILY
- LINGER/FINISH

RATING

☆ ☆ ☆ ☆ ☆

FLAVOR STRENGTH

- FULL
- MED. FULL
- MEDIUM
- MILD
- MELLOW

NOTES

_____

_____

_____

_____

_____

NAME OF CIGAR _____

BRAND _____ ORIGIN _____

PRICE _____ DATE _____

LENGTH/RING SIZE _____ / _____ BUY AGAIN? _____

AFFIX LABEL HERE

FLAVOR WHEEL

- BODY
- DARK FRUIT
- TROPICAL FRUIT
- HERBAL
- SPICY
- SWEET
- VANILLA
- TOFFEE
- CHOCOLATE
- NUTTY
- WOODY
- EARTHY
- LEATHER
- BITTER
- OILY
- LINGER/FINISH

RATING

☆☆☆☆☆

FLAVOR STRENGTH

- FULL
- MED. FULL
- MEDIUM
- MILD
- MELLOW

NOTES

_____

_____

_____

_____

_____

NAME OF CIGAR _____

BRAND _____ ORIGIN _____

PRICE _____ DATE _____

LENGTH/RING SIZE _____ / _____ BUY AGAIN? _____

AFFIX LABEL HERE

FLAVOR WHEEL

- BODY
- LINGER/FINISH
- OILY
- BITTER
- LEATHER
- EARTHY
- WOODY
- NUTTY
- CHOCOLATE
- TOFFEE
- VANILLA
- SWEET
- SPICY
- HERBAL
- TROPICAL FRUIT
- DARK FRUIT

RATING
☆ ☆ ☆ ☆ ☆

FLAVOR STRENGTH
- FULL
- MED. FULL
- MEDIUM
- MILD
- MELLOW

NOTES
_____
_____
_____
_____
_____

NAME OF CIGAR _____

BRAND _____ ORIGIN _____

PRICE _____ DATE _____

LENGTH/RING SIZE _____ / _____ BUY AGAIN? _____

AFFIX LABEL HERE

FLAVOR WHEEL

- BODY
- DARK FRUIT
- TROPICAL FRUIT
- HERBAL
- SPICY
- SWEET
- VANILLA
- TOFFEE
- CHOCOLATE
- NUTTY
- WOODY
- EARTHY
- LEATHER
- BITTER
- OILY
- LINGER/FINISH

RATING

☆ ☆ ☆ ☆ ☆

FLAVOR STRENGTH

- FULL
- MED. FULL
- MEDIUM
- MILD
- MELLOW

NOTES

_____
_____
_____
_____
_____

NAME OF CIGAR _____

BRAND _____ ORIGIN _____

PRICE _____ DATE _____

LENGTH/RING SIZE _____ / _____ BUY AGAIN? _____

AFFIX LABEL HERE

FLAVOR WHEEL

- BODY
- DARK FRUIT
- TROPICAL FRUIT
- HERBAL
- SPICY
- SWEET
- VANILLA
- TOFFEE
- CHOCOLATE
- NUTTY
- WOODY
- EARTHY
- LEATHER
- BITTER
- OILY
- LINGER/FINISH

RATING

☆☆☆☆☆

FLAVOR STRENGTH

- FULL
- MED. FULL
- MEDIUM
- MILD
- MELLOW

NOTES

_____

_____

_____

_____

_____

NAME OF CIGAR _____

BRAND _____ ORIGIN _____

PRICE _____ DATE _____

LENGTH/RING SIZE _____ / _____ BUY AGAIN? _____

AFFIX LABEL HERE

FLAVOR WHEEL

Flavor wheel axes: BODY, DARK FRUIT, TROPICAL FRUIT, HERBAL, SPICY, SWEET, VANILLA, TOFFEE, CHOCOLATE, NUTTY, WOODY, EARTHY, LEATHER, BITTER, OILY, LINGER/FINISH (scale 0–5)

RATING
☆☆☆☆☆

FLAVOR STRENGTH
- FULL
- MED. FULL
- MEDIUM
- MILD
- MELLOW

NOTES

_____
_____
_____
_____
_____

NAME OF CIGAR _____

BRAND _____ ORIGIN _____

PRICE _____ DATE _____

LENGTH/RING SIZE _____ / _____ BUY AGAIN? _____

AFFIX LABEL HERE

FLAVOR WHEEL

- BODY
- LINGER/FINISH
- OILY
- BITTER
- LEATHER
- EARTHY
- WOODY
- NUTTY
- CHOCOLATE
- TOFFEE
- VANILLA
- SWEET
- SPICY
- HERBAL
- TROPICAL FRUIT
- DARK FRUIT

RATING

☆ ☆ ☆ ☆ ☆

FLAVOR STRENGTH

- FULL
- MED. FULL
- MEDIUM
- MILD
- MELLOW

NOTES

_____

_____

_____

_____

_____

NAME OF CIGAR ______________________________

BRAND ______________________ ORIGIN ______________

PRICE ______________________ DATE ______________

LENGTH/RING SIZE _______/_______ BUY AGAIN? ______________

AFFIX LABEL HERE

FLAVOR WHEEL

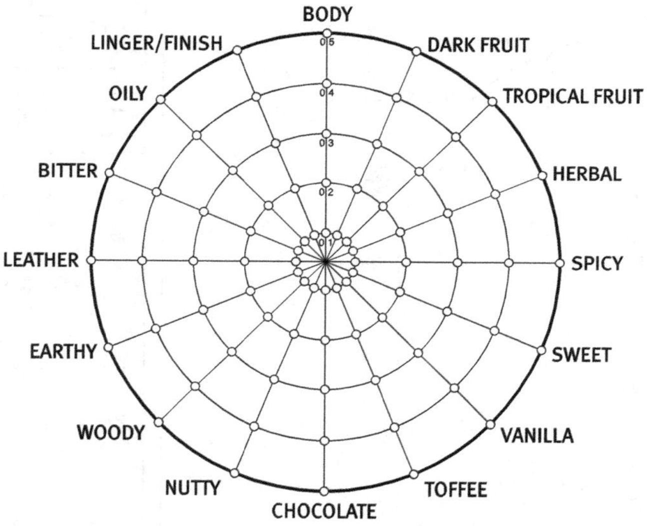

BODY
DARK FRUIT
TROPICAL FRUIT
HERBAL
SPICY
SWEET
VANILLA
TOFFEE
CHOCOLATE
NUTTY
WOODY
EARTHY
LEATHER
BITTER
OILY
LINGER/FINISH

RATING

☆☆☆☆☆

FLAVOR STRENGTH

FULL

MED. FULL

MEDIUM

MILD

MELLOW

NOTES

____

____

____

____

____

NAME OF CIGAR _____

BRAND _____ ORIGIN _____

PRICE _____ DATE _____

LENGTH/RING SIZE _____ / _____ BUY AGAIN? _____

AFFIX LABEL HERE

FLAVOR WHEEL

- BODY
- DARK FRUIT
- TROPICAL FRUIT
- HERBAL
- SPICY
- SWEET
- VANILLA
- TOFFEE
- CHOCOLATE
- NUTTY
- WOODY
- EARTHY
- LEATHER
- BITTER
- OILY
- LINGER/FINISH

RATING

☆ ☆ ☆ ☆ ☆

FLAVOR STRENGTH

- FULL
- MED. FULL
- MEDIUM
- MILD
- MELLOW

NOTES

_____

_____

_____

_____

_____

NAME OF CIGAR _____

BRAND _____ ORIGIN _____

PRICE _____ DATE _____

LENGTH/RING SIZE _____ / _____ BUY AGAIN? _____

```
AFFIX LABEL HERE
```

FLAVOR WHEEL

- BODY
- LINGER/FINISH
- OILY
- BITTER
- LEATHER
- EARTHY
- WOODY
- NUTTY
- CHOCOLATE
- TOFFEE
- VANILLA
- SWEET
- SPICY
- HERBAL
- TROPICAL FRUIT
- DARK FRUIT

RATING

☆ ☆ ☆ ☆ ☆

FLAVOR STRENGTH

- FULL
- MED. FULL
- MEDIUM
- MILD
- MELLOW

NOTES

_____

_____

_____

_____

_____

NAME OF CIGAR _____

BRAND _____ ORIGIN _____

PRICE _____ DATE _____

LENGTH/RING SIZE _____ / _____ BUY AGAIN? _____

AFFIX LABEL HERE

FLAVOR WHEEL

- BODY
- DARK FRUIT
- TROPICAL FRUIT
- HERBAL
- SPICY
- SWEET
- VANILLA
- TOFFEE
- CHOCOLATE
- NUTTY
- WOODY
- EARTHY
- LEATHER
- BITTER
- OILY
- LINGER/FINISH

RATING

☆ ☆ ☆ ☆ ☆

FLAVOR STRENGTH

- FULL
- MED. FULL
- MEDIUM
- MILD
- MELLOW

NOTES

_____

_____

_____

_____

NAME OF CIGAR _____

BRAND _____ ORIGIN _____

PRICE _____ DATE _____

LENGTH/RING SIZE _____ / _____ BUY AGAIN? _____

[AFFIX LABEL HERE]

FLAVOR WHEEL

- BODY
- DARK FRUIT
- TROPICAL FRUIT
- HERBAL
- SPICY
- SWEET
- VANILLA
- TOFFEE
- CHOCOLATE
- NUTTY
- WOODY
- EARTHY
- LEATHER
- BITTER
- OILY
- LINGER/FINISH

RATING

☆☆☆☆☆

FLAVOR STRENGTH

- FULL
- MED. FULL
- MEDIUM
- MILD
- MELLOW

NOTES

_____
_____
_____
_____
_____

NAME OF CIGAR _____

BRAND _____ ORIGIN _____

PRICE _____ DATE _____

LENGTH/RING SIZE _____ / _____ BUY AGAIN? _____

AFFIX LABEL HERE

FLAVOR WHEEL

- BODY
- LINGER/FINISH
- DARK FRUIT
- OILY
- TROPICAL FRUIT
- BITTER
- HERBAL
- LEATHER
- SPICY
- EARTHY
- SWEET
- WOODY
- VANILLA
- NUTTY
- TOFFEE
- CHOCOLATE

RATING

☆ ☆ ☆ ☆ ☆

FLAVOR STRENGTH

- FULL
- MED. FULL
- MEDIUM
- MILD
- MELLOW

NOTES

_____

_____

_____

_____

_____

NAME OF CIGAR _____

BRAND _____ ORIGIN _____

PRICE _____ DATE _____

LENGTH/RING SIZE _____ / _____ BUY AGAIN? _____

AFFIX LABEL HERE

FLAVOR WHEEL

- BODY
- DARK FRUIT
- TROPICAL FRUIT
- HERBAL
- SPICY
- SWEET
- VANILLA
- TOFFEE
- CHOCOLATE
- NUTTY
- WOODY
- EARTHY
- LEATHER
- BITTER
- OILY
- LINGER/FINISH

RATING

☆ ☆ ☆ ☆ ☆

FLAVOR STRENGTH

- FULL
- MED. FULL
- MEDIUM
- MILD
- MELLOW

NOTES

_____

_____

_____

_____

_____

NAME OF CIGAR _____

BRAND _____ ORIGIN _____

PRICE _____ DATE _____

LENGTH/RING SIZE _____ / _____ BUY AGAIN? _____

AFFIX LABEL HERE

FLAVOR WHEEL

- BODY
- DARK FRUIT
- TROPICAL FRUIT
- HERBAL
- SPICY
- SWEET
- VANILLA
- TOFFEE
- CHOCOLATE
- NUTTY
- WOODY
- EARTHY
- LEATHER
- BITTER
- OILY
- LINGER/FINISH

RATING

☆ ☆ ☆ ☆ ☆

FLAVOR STRENGTH

- FULL
- MED. FULL
- MEDIUM
- MILD
- MELLOW

NOTES

_____

_____

_____

_____

_____

NAME OF CIGAR ______________________

BRAND ______________________ ORIGIN ______________________

PRICE ______________________ DATE ______________________

LENGTH/RING SIZE ________/________ BUY AGAIN? ______________________

AFFIX LABEL HERE

FLAVOR WHEEL

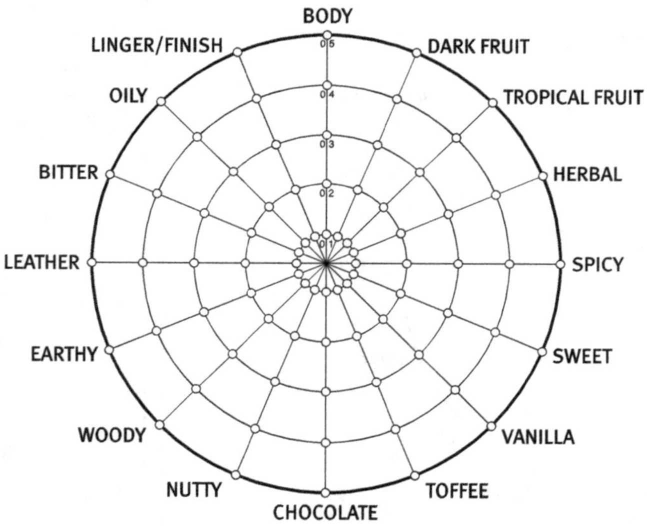

BODY
DARK FRUIT
TROPICAL FRUIT
HERBAL
SPICY
SWEET
VANILLA
TOFFEE
CHOCOLATE
NUTTY
WOODY
EARTHY
LEATHER
BITTER
OILY
LINGER/FINISH

RATING

☆☆☆☆☆

FLAVOR STRENGTH

FULL
MED. FULL
MEDIUM
MILD
MELLOW

NOTES

____

____

____

____

____

NAME OF CIGAR ______________________________

BRAND ______________________ ORIGIN ______________________

PRICE ______________________ DATE ______________________

LENGTH/RING SIZE _______/_______ BUY AGAIN? ______________________

AFFIX LABEL HERE

FLAVOR WHEEL

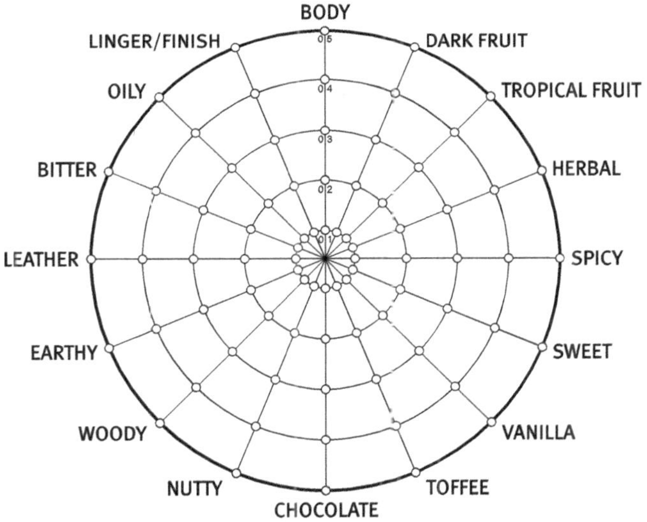
BODY
DARK FRUIT
TROPICAL FRUIT
HERBAL
SPICY
SWEET
VANILLA
TOFFEE
CHOCOLATE
NUTTY
WOODY
EARTHY
LEATHER
BITTER
OILY
LINGER/FINISH

RATING

☆☆☆☆☆

FLAVOR STRENGTH

FULL
MED. FULL
MEDIUM
MILD
MELLOW

NOTES

____

____

____

____

____

NAME OF CIGAR _____

BRAND _____ ORIGIN _____

PRICE _____ DATE _____

LENGTH/RING SIZE _____ / _____ BUY AGAIN? _____

AFFIX LABEL HERE

FLAVOR WHEEL

- BODY
- DARK FRUIT
- TROPICAL FRUIT
- HERBAL
- SPICY
- SWEET
- VANILLA
- TOFFEE
- CHOCOLATE
- NUTTY
- WOODY
- EARTHY
- LEATHER
- BITTER
- OILY
- LINGER/FINISH

RATING

☆ ☆ ☆ ☆ ☆

FLAVOR STRENGTH

- FULL
- MED. FULL
- MEDIUM
- MILD
- MELLOW

NOTES

_____

_____

_____

_____

_____

NAME OF CIGAR _____

BRAND _____ ORIGIN _____

PRICE _____ DATE _____

LENGTH/RING SIZE _____ / _____ BUY AGAIN? _____

AFFIX LABEL HERE

FLAVOR WHEEL

- BODY
- LINGER/FINISH
- DARK FRUIT
- OILY
- TROPICAL FRUIT
- BITTER
- HERBAL
- LEATHER
- SPICY
- EARTHY
- SWEET
- WOODY
- VANILLA
- NUTTY
- TOFFEE
- CHOCOLATE

RATING

☆ ☆ ☆ ☆ ☆

FLAVOR STRENGTH

- FULL
- MED. FULL
- MEDIUM
- MILD
- MELLOW

NOTES

NAME OF CIGAR _____

BRAND _____ ORIGIN _____

PRICE _____ DATE _____

LENGTH/RING SIZE _____ / _____ BUY AGAIN? _____

AFFIX LABEL HERE

FLAVOR WHEEL

- BODY
- DARK FRUIT
- TROPICAL FRUIT
- HERBAL
- SPICY
- SWEET
- VANILLA
- TOFFEE
- CHOCOLATE
- NUTTY
- WOODY
- EARTHY
- LEATHER
- BITTER
- OILY
- LINGER/FINISH

RATING

☆ ☆ ☆ ☆ ☆

FLAVOR STRENGTH

- FULL
- MED. FULL
- MEDIUM
- MILD
- MELLOW

NOTES

_____

_____

_____

_____

_____

NAME OF CIGAR _____

BRAND _____ ORIGIN _____

PRICE _____ DATE _____

LENGTH/RING SIZE _____ / _____ BUY AGAIN? _____

AFFIX LABEL HERE

FLAVOR WHEEL

- BODY
- DARK FRUIT
- TROPICAL FRUIT
- HERBAL
- SPICY
- SWEET
- VANILLA
- TOFFEE
- CHOCOLATE
- NUTTY
- WOODY
- EARTHY
- LEATHER
- BITTER
- OILY
- LINGER/FINISH

RATING

☆☆☆☆☆

FLAVOR STRENGTH

- FULL
- MED. FULL
- MEDIUM
- MILD
- MELLOW

NOTES

_____
_____
_____
_____
_____

NAME OF CIGAR _____

BRAND _____ ORIGIN _____

PRICE _____ DATE _____

LENGTH/RING SIZE _____ / _____ BUY AGAIN? _____

AFFIX LABEL HERE

FLAVOR WHEEL

- BODY
- DARK FRUIT
- TROPICAL FRUIT
- HERBAL
- SPICY
- SWEET
- VANILLA
- TOFFEE
- CHOCOLATE
- NUTTY
- WOODY
- EARTHY
- LEATHER
- BITTER
- OILY
- LINGER/FINISH

RATING

☆ ☆ ☆ ☆ ☆

FLAVOR STRENGTH

- FULL
- MED. FULL
- MEDIUM
- MILD
- MELLOW

NOTES

_____

_____

_____

_____

_____

NAME OF CIGAR _____

BRAND _____ ORIGIN _____

PRICE _____ DATE _____

LENGTH/RING SIZE _____/_____ BUY AGAIN? _____

```
┌─────────────────────────────────────────────┐
│               AFFIX LABEL HERE              │
└─────────────────────────────────────────────┘
```

FLAVOR WHEEL

Flavor wheel axes: BODY, DARK FRUIT, TROPICAL FRUIT, HERBAL, SPICY, SWEET, VANILLA, TOFFEE, CHOCOLATE, NUTTY, WOODY, EARTHY, LEATHER, BITTER, OILY, LINGER/FINISH

RATING

☆ ☆ ☆ ☆ ☆

FLAVOR STRENGTH

- FULL
- MED. FULL
- MEDIUM
- MILD
- MELLOW

NOTES

_____

_____

_____

_____

_____

NAME OF CIGAR _____

BRAND _____ ORIGIN _____

PRICE _____ DATE _____

LENGTH/RING SIZE _____/_____ BUY AGAIN? _____

AFFIX LABEL HERE

FLAVOR WHEEL

- BODY
- DARK FRUIT
- TROPICAL FRUIT
- HERBAL
- SPICY
- SWEET
- VANILLA
- TOFFEE
- CHOCOLATE
- NUTTY
- WOODY
- EARTHY
- LEATHER
- BITTER
- OILY
- LINGER/FINISH

RATING
☆ ☆ ☆ ☆ ☆

FLAVOR STRENGTH
- FULL
- MED. FULL
- MEDIUM
- MILD
- MELLOW

NOTES
_____
_____
_____
_____
_____

NAME OF CIGAR _____

BRAND _____ ORIGIN _____

PRICE _____ DATE _____

LENGTH/RING SIZE _____ / _____ BUY AGAIN? _____

AFFIX LABEL HERE

FLAVOR WHEEL

- BODY
- DARK FRUIT
- TROPICAL FRUIT
- HERBAL
- SPICY
- SWEET
- VANILLA
- TOFFEE
- CHOCOLATE
- NUTTY
- WOODY
- EARTHY
- LEATHER
- BITTER
- OILY
- LINGER/FINISH

RATING

☆☆☆☆☆

FLAVOR STRENGTH

- FULL
- MED. FULL
- MEDIUM
- MILD
- MELLOW

NOTES

_____

_____

_____

_____

_____

NAME OF CIGAR _____

BRAND _____ ORIGIN _____

PRICE _____ DATE _____

LENGTH/RING SIZE _____ / _____ BUY AGAIN? _____

AFFIX LABEL HERE

FLAVOR WHEEL

- BODY
- LINGER/FINISH
- OILY
- BITTER
- LEATHER
- EARTHY
- WOODY
- NUTTY
- CHOCOLATE
- TOFFEE
- VANILLA
- SWEET
- SPICY
- HERBAL
- TROPICAL FRUIT
- DARK FRUIT

RATING

☆ ☆ ☆ ☆ ☆

FLAVOR STRENGTH

- FULL
- MED. FULL
- MEDIUM
- MILD
- MELLOW

NOTES

NAME OF CIGAR _____

BRAND _____ ORIGIN _____

PRICE _____ DATE _____

LENGTH/RING SIZE _____ / _____ BUY AGAIN? _____

AFFIX LABEL HERE

FLAVOR WHEEL

- BODY
- DARK FRUIT
- TROPICAL FRUIT
- HERBAL
- SPICY
- SWEET
- VANILLA
- TOFFEE
- CHOCOLATE
- NUTTY
- WOODY
- EARTHY
- LEATHER
- BITTER
- OILY
- LINGER/FINISH

RATING

☆ ☆ ☆ ☆ ☆

FLAVOR STRENGTH

- FULL
- MED. FULL
- MEDIUM
- MILD
- MELLOW

NOTES

_____

_____

_____

_____

NAME OF CIGAR _____

BRAND _____ ORIGIN _____

PRICE _____ DATE _____

LENGTH/RING SIZE _____ / _____ BUY AGAIN? _____

AFFIX LABEL HERE

FLAVOR WHEEL

- BODY
- LINGER/FINISH
- OILY
- BITTER
- LEATHER
- EARTHY
- WOODY
- NUTTY
- CHOCOLATE
- TOFFEE
- VANILLA
- SWEET
- SPICY
- HERBAL
- TROPICAL FRUIT
- DARK FRUIT

RATING

☆ ☆ ☆ ☆ ☆

FLAVOR STRENGTH

- FULL
- MED. FULL
- MEDIUM
- MILD
- MELLOW

NOTES

_____
_____
_____
_____
_____

NAME OF CIGAR _____

BRAND _____ ORIGIN _____

PRICE _____ DATE _____

LENGTH/RING SIZE _____ / _____ BUY AGAIN? _____

AFFIX LABEL HERE

FLAVOR WHEEL

- BODY
- LINGER/FINISH
- DARK FRUIT
- OILY
- TROPICAL FRUIT
- BITTER
- HERBAL
- LEATHER
- SPICY
- EARTHY
- SWEET
- WOODY
- VANILLA
- NUTTY
- TOFFEE
- CHOCOLATE

RATING

☆ ☆ ☆ ☆ ☆

FLAVOR STRENGTH

- FULL
- MED. FULL
- MEDIUM
- MILD
- MELLOW

NOTES

_____

_____

_____

_____

_____

NAME OF CIGAR _____

BRAND _____ ORIGIN _____

PRICE _____ DATE _____

LENGTH/RING SIZE _____ / _____ BUY AGAIN? _____

AFFIX LABEL HERE

FLAVOR WHEEL

- BODY
- DARK FRUIT
- TROPICAL FRUIT
- HERBAL
- SPICY
- SWEET
- VANILLA
- TOFFEE
- CHOCOLATE
- NUTTY
- WOODY
- EARTHY
- LEATHER
- BITTER
- OILY
- LINGER/FINISH

RATING

☆☆☆☆☆

FLAVOR STRENGTH

- FULL
- MED. FULL
- MEDIUM
- MILD
- MELLOW

NOTES

_____

_____

_____

_____

_____

NAME OF CIGAR _____

BRAND _____ ORIGIN _____

PRICE _____ DATE _____

LENGTH/RING SIZE _____ / _____ BUY AGAIN? _____

AFFIX LABEL HERE

FLAVOR WHEEL

- BODY
- LINGER/FINISH
- DARK FRUIT
- OILY
- TROPICAL FRUIT
- BITTER
- HERBAL
- LEATHER
- SPICY
- EARTHY
- SWEET
- WOODY
- VANILLA
- NUTTY
- TOFFEE
- CHOCOLATE

RATING

☆ ☆ ☆ ☆ ☆

FLAVOR STRENGTH

- FULL
- MED. FULL
- MEDIUM
- MILD
- MELLOW

NOTES

_____

_____

_____

_____

_____

NAME OF CIGAR _____

BRAND _____ ORIGIN _____

PRICE _____ DATE _____

LENGTH/RING SIZE _____ / _____ BUY AGAIN? _____

AFFIX LABEL HERE

FLAVOR WHEEL

- BODY
- DARK FRUIT
- TROPICAL FRUIT
- HERBAL
- SPICY
- SWEET
- VANILLA
- TOFFEE
- CHOCOLATE
- NUTTY
- WOODY
- EARTHY
- LEATHER
- BITTER
- OILY
- LINGER/FINISH

RATING

☆ ☆ ☆ ☆ ☆

FLAVOR STRENGTH

- FULL
- MED. FULL
- MEDIUM
- MILD
- MELLOW

NOTES

_____

_____

_____

_____

_____

NAME OF CIGAR _____

BRAND _____ ORIGIN _____

PRICE _____ DATE _____

LENGTH/RING SIZE _____/_____ BUY AGAIN? _____

AFFIX LABEL HERE

FLAVOR WHEEL

- BODY
- DARK FRUIT
- TROPICAL FRUIT
- HERBAL
- SPICY
- SWEET
- VANILLA
- TOFFEE
- CHOCOLATE
- NUTTY
- WOODY
- EARTHY
- LEATHER
- BITTER
- OILY
- LINGER/FINISH

RATING

☆ ☆ ☆ ☆ ☆

FLAVOR STRENGTH

- FULL
- MED. FULL
- MEDIUM
- MILD
- MELLOW

NOTES

_____
_____
_____
_____
_____

NAME OF CIGAR _____

BRAND _____ ORIGIN _____

PRICE _____ DATE _____

LENGTH/RING SIZE _____ / _____ BUY AGAIN? _____

AFFIX LABEL HERE

FLAVOR WHEEL

- BODY
- DARK FRUIT
- TROPICAL FRUIT
- HERBAL
- SPICY
- SWEET
- VANILLA
- TOFFEE
- CHOCOLATE
- NUTTY
- WOODY
- EARTHY
- LEATHER
- BITTER
- OILY
- LINGER/FINISH

RATING

☆ ☆ ☆ ☆ ☆

FLAVOR STRENGTH

- FULL
- MED. FULL
- MEDIUM
- MILD
- MELLOW

NOTES

_____

_____

_____

_____

_____

www.ingramcontent.com/pod-product-compliance
Lightning Source LLC
Chambersburg PA
CBHW081231080526
44587CB00022B/3903